# THANKS FOR TELLING ME

## CHARLEE KING

WWW.SELFPUBLISHN30DAYS.COM

Published by Self Publish -N- 30 Days

Copyright 2019 Charlee King.

All rights reserved worldwide. No part of this book may be reproduced or transmitted in any form or by any means electronic or mechanical, including photocopying, recording or by any information storage and retrieval system without written permission from Charlee King.

Printed in the United States of America

ISBN: 978-1-64007-745-4 1. Motherhood 2. Child Care Charlee King

Thanks for Telling Me

Disclaimer/Warning:

This book is intended for lecture and informative purposes only. The author or publisher does not guarantee that anyone following these steps will be successful in motherhood or parenting. The author and publisher shall have neither liability responsibility to anyone with respect to any loss or damage cause, or alleged to be caused, directly or indirectly by the information contained in this book.

*This book is dedicated to my daughter Bianca.
You are the reason I smile and you have made me
a better person.*

# TABLE OF CONTENTS

*Acknowledgments* ........................... ix

*Chapter 1: Postpartum Constipation* .......... 1

*Chapter 2: Hair Loss* ....................... 9

*Chapter 3: Post Baby Belly* ................. 17

*Chapter 4: Feet Growth* ..................... 25

*Chapter 5: Skin Change* ..................... 33

*Chapter 6: Postpartum Depression* ........... 41

*Chapter 7: Postpartum Bleeding* ............. 49

*Chapter 8: Breast Growth/Lactation* ......... 57

*Chapter 9: Breastfeeding* ................... 65

*Chapter 10: Sweating* ....................... 83

*Chapter 11: Sleep* .......................... 91

*Chapter 12: Sex Drive* ...................... 97

*Chapter 13: Dental* ......................... 105

*Chapter 14: Bladder* ........................ 115

*References* ................................. 121

*About the Author* ........................... 125

# MOMMY'S SWEET TREATS
## Gourmet Lactation Cookies

Great for Mom and Dad to eat them too!!
www.mommyssweettreats.com

@mommyssweettreats

@mommyssweetcookies

# *Acknowledgments*

Thank you to all my friends and family who have supported me and believed in me.

Harry Cunningham
Pam Hawthorne-Tatum
Shandai Sams
Dr. Jessika Mayes
Stephen F. Austin State University
Texas Southern University
Bianca Carter
Sharon Tarrant
Virgil Gray Sr.
Ola Mae Gray

SILENCE IS GOLDEN...
UNLESS YOU HAVE KIDS,
THEN IT'S JUST SUSPICIOUS.

# CHAPTER 1
## *Postpartum Constipation*

CONSTIPATION AND PROCRASTINATION ARE SIMILAR.
IN BOTH CONDITIONS, YOU DON'T A GIVE A CRAP.

Have you ever heard the saying, "Don't write a check that your ass can't cash?" Well, this is one case where that statement rings true. Let's just say you will give birth twice, once to your baby, then to a baseball. Unlike labor pains, symptoms of constipation is something mothers may not be expecting.

It's not uncommon for moms to deal with constipation after birth. Constipation is just something most postpartum mothers endure during recovery. For some, they may be surprised to be dealing with constipation after a pregnancy where it had not been an issue before. For others, constipation is nothing new. If you had a long labor without eating anything, or if you had a bowel movement or an enema during labor, it may be a day or two until you're back to normal because there simply isn't anything in your intestines. And if you had a c-section, it can take three or four days for your bowels to start functioning as usual. Though constipation is normal, it can be annoying. Discomfort can be caused by one of the several factors relating to what was happening to your body before, during, and/or after delivery.

**It can be factors such as:**

1. You had a long labor with little food.
2. You had a bowel movement or enema during labor.
3. You had a c-section. It can take up to 3–4 days for your digestive system to start working normally following this major surgery.
4. You used pain relievers during delivery, or you are using them currently for postpartum pain relief. Systemic narcotics, in particular, can slow down the digestive tract.
5. You have a sore perineum possibly caused by an episiotomy or by postpartum hemorrhoids. In this case, and most likely, the constipation is not so much a physical problem as a mental one.

## POSTPARTUM CONSTIPATION

You may be afraid of tearing your stitches or more pain. That fear is causing you to retain your stool.

Depending on the root cause of your constipation and the steps you take to treat it, it is very likely that it will be resolved within a few days of giving birth. The important thing is to be proactive in treating constipation and follow the steps below. Constipation is usually not serious, but occasionally it can be a symptom of another problem. Call your healthcare provider immediately if you have mucus or blood in your stool, or if you have severe constipation that is accompanied by abdominal pain and alternates with diarrhea.

**Some tips for preventing and easing constipation:**

1. Don't wait to go to the bathroom when you feel the urge to move your bowels, even though it might be uncomfortable the first few times. Waiting makes your stool drier and harder to pass.
2. Eat high-fiber foods, such as whole grain cereals and breads, brown rice, and beans, as well as fresh fruits and vegetables every day.
3. Carry a water bottle and drink plenty of water. A daily glass of fruit juice, especially prune juice, can also be helpful. Some people find that drinking warm liquid soon after waking up helps get things moving.
4. Go for a walk. Walking may be painful at first, especially if you're recovering from a c-section or an episiotomy, but even a short trip around the block can get your sluggish bowels into gear.
5. Ask your healthcare provider whether you should take a stool softener or laxative, sold over the counter at any drugstore. Stool softeners enhance water absorption in the stool, while laxatives stimulate the stool to pass. You'll need to start taking a stool softener right away if you have a tear that extends into or through

your sphincter. Stool softeners are also helpful if you're suffering from hemorrhoids or taking high-dose iron supplements for anemia or narcotics for pain relief.

6. If things don't improve in a few days, talk with your healthcare provider. She may have additional recommendations for you to try, or she may need to do a manual decompaction, which is a procedure to break up the hardened stool with a gloved and lubricated finger.

Also, straining during a bowel movement or passing a hard stool can cause or worsen hemorrhoids. Hemorrhoids may shrink quickly, or they may persist for months postpartum. Sometimes hemorrhoid symptoms may wax and wane for years. Although hemorrhoids can be extremely uncomfortable, they rarely lead to serious problems. Even if your constipation doesn't seem serious, don't hesitate to discuss it with your healthcare provider if it persists.

"BUT MOM...WHAT IF I GET KIDNAPPED?"
"TRUST ME, THEY'LL BRING YOU BACK."

# CHAPTER 2
## *Hair Loss*

SUDDENLY YOU'RE LIKE, "WHO THE HELL TOOK MY HAIR?" THEN YOU LOOK DOWN AND REALIZE YOUR PILLOW IS THE CULPRIT.

**T**here were some things that I was expecting to happen after giving birth, and pulling my hair out was one of those things. I thought it would be from not having enough sleep, the baby constantly crying, or me realizing what an awful choice I made in having a baby with the man I did. You know, normal stuff. I never thought that merely giving birth would cause me to lose my hair.

Your hormones change dramatically during pregnancy. Immediately after your baby is born, several of your hormone levels drop quickly, including estrogen and progesterone. Hormones are the biggest reason for your pregnancy hair changes and postpartum hair loss. Your high levels of estrogen while pregnant prevented your usual rate of hair loss. Normally, your hair falls out in small amounts every day. During pregnancy, your hair loss decreases. The effect is compounded by your increased blood volume and circulation, which also causes your hair to fall out less than normal.

After your baby arrives and your hormone levels drop, your hair makes up for lost time by falling out in much bigger clumps than it normally does. The total volume of your hair loss probably isn't more than you would have lost over the last nine months, it just seems like it because it's happening all at once. Like me, many new moms are surprised to be shedding more hair than usual in the first few months after giving birth, but it's perfectly normal. And there's no need to panic: Your hair should be back to normal around your baby's first birthday. Normally between 85 and 95 percent of the hair on your head is actively growing, while the other 5 to 15 percent is in a resting stage. After the resting period, this hair falls out—often while you're brushing or shampooing it—and is replaced by new growth. The average woman sheds about 100 hairs a day.

Postpartum hair loss can set in any day after your baby arrives, and it sometimes continues as long as a year. It usually peaks around the 4-month mark, so if your baby is a few months old and you're still losing clumps of hair, that doesn't mean it's time to panic! It's normal for your hair to thin out after pregnancy. If it's not worrying you, you don't need to do anything to treat it. And, unfortunately, there is nothing that has been shown to prevent or slow postpartum hair loss. But if your hair loss is bothering you, there are treatments you can try to make your hair appear fuller and healthier.

**Postpartum hair treatments to try:**

*1. Skip the styling.*
Heating your hair with a dryer or curling iron may make it look thinner. Try to hold off on fancy styling and let your hair air-dry until the thinning tapers out.

Brushing too hard can also cause your hair to fall out in bigger clumps, so be gentle when brushing and don't brush more than once a day. You can use the extra time to cuddle your baby or catch up on sleep!

*2. Eat well.*
Including a variety of fruits, vegetables, and healthy proteins in your diet is the best way to make sure your body is getting all the nutrients it needs.

Foods that are suggested by some to improve hair health include dark leafy greens (for the iron and vitamin C), sweet potatoes and carrots (for the beta carotene), eggs (for the vitamin D), and fish (for omega-3s and magnesium).

*3. Take your vitamins.*
Vitamins shouldn't be a substitute for a varied diet, especially when you're a new mom with a baby to take care of. But they may help as a supplement if your diet is not well-balanced. While no specific vitamins have been shown to affect hair loss, they are important for overall health. It is often recommended to continue your prenatal vitamins after your baby is born, especially if you are breast-feeding.

***4. Use volumizing shampoo.***
While there's no evidence for it, conditioning shampoos sometimes weigh your hair down and make it look thinner and limper. Volumizers may add body to your hair and help you maintain a lustrous look. In most cases, your postpartum hair loss is totally normal and not anything to worry about. If you're still seeing clumps in your hairbrush after your baby hits their 1st birthday, you may want to talk to a dermatologist to make sure there isn't an additional cause for your hair loss.

Not all women notice dramatic changes in their hair during pregnancy or the postpartum period, but it tends to be more obvious among women with longer hair. It's worth talking with your healthcare provider about your hair loss if you think it's excessive. Hair loss can be a symptom of anemia or postpartum thyroiditis, which are treatable conditions. You won't be able to prevent the hair from falling out, but you can experiment with different products (such as hair thickener or mousse) to give your hair a fuller look during this transition period.

Avoid heavy conditioners, which tend to weigh down hair. If you're tired of scooping hair out of the shower drain or sweeping strands off the bathroom floor, you may want to opt for a short hair cut. Plus, a short, wash-and-go hairstyle can be easier to manage when you have a new baby in the house and you're strapped for time.

**Note:** If you have long hair, strands of it can end up tightly wrapped around your baby's tiny appendages, including his fingers, toes, wrists, ankles, and penis. This is called a hair tourniquet and it can be quite painful for your little one. If he's ever crying for no apparent reason, check carefully for tight bands of hair.

YOU KNOW YOU'RE A MOM WHEN... PICKING UP ANOTHER HUMAN TO SMELL THEIR BUTT IS NOT ONLY NORMAL BUT ALSO TOTALLY NECESSARY.

# CHAPTER 3
## *Post Baby Belly*

A mother noticed her daughter's stomach bulging and immediately asked her, "Cindy! How did you get pregnant?! Didn't I tell you to say "DON'T" if a man touches your breast, and say "STOP" if he touches your private?"

The daughter replied, "Yes mom, I did that, but he was touching both at the same time and I had to say, "DON'T STOP!"

## THANKS FOR TELLING ME

You've had a baby and your belly is probably showing the signs. Although stretch marks, loose skin, and a squishy tummy are all normal and common after pregnancy, as are c-section scars, we all can't wait to get our post-body back. I gave birth in February and wanted to be beach ready by the summer. I bought all the exercise videos I could and was challenging myself to do 200 crunches a day. Sounds realistic right? Well, I have a spoiler alert. Crunches are as ineffective as they are dull for toning your ab muscles. In fact, working only the outer abdominal muscles as crunches do, without strengthening the underlying ones first, can actually make your pooch worse.

After delivering a baby, whether that be vaginally or via caesarian, your body is going to need some time to heal. Most doctors will clear you for exercise on average 6–8 weeks postpartum, but your body will still need some time to ease back into it. It took your body nine months to grow a human being and you should give it at least that long, ideally longer, to return to its new normal. While there are women who get back into their pre-pregnancy jeans a week after giving birth, that is definitely not the norm.

The most common reason women struggle to get a flat stomach after having a baby is due to an issue known as diastasis recti. Diastasis recti occurs when the tissue that holds your abdominal muscles together stretches or rips.

Another common problem is an issue with your pelvic floor. It's not as commonly discussed as diastasis recti is becoming, but still equally, if not more, important. The pelvic floor affects things like urination and the ability to hold your internal organs up and in. Some may suffer from a cystocele, which is when your bladder is LITERALLY falling out of your body. It's very important to realize the intense impact giving birth can have on a woman's body.

# POST BABY BELLY

## Exercises to help heal postpartum body:

### *1. Pelvic Tilt*
Do this move as early as one week after you have your baby if you had a vaginal delivery; if you had a C-section you might have to wait 8–10 weeks. Lie on your back with your knees bent and a pillow under your hips and another between your knees. Feet flat and your arms at your sides, inhale, then exhale and draw your abs in and tuck your pelvis under slightly, squeezing your buttocks as you do a Kegel. Hold 5 seconds and release for 10 reps.

Benefits: Improves deep abdominal strength and stamina.

### *2. Pelvic Bridge*
After six weeks, add this move to your routine. Lie on your back with feet hip-width apart, knees bent. Inhale, then exhale as you draw your abs up and in toward your spine. Tilt your pelvis up, lifting your hips off the floor into a bridge. Slowly lower down to starting position. Repeat 5 times, building up to 10.

Benefits: Strengthens the transverse, buttocks and lower back.

### *3. Heel Slides*
Lie on your back with your knees bent, feet hip-width apart and abs drawn in. Flex your left foot, pressing your heel into the floor. Keeping your pelvis still, inhale, then exhale as you use your deep abdominal muscles to push your left heel away from your body, keeping the knee slightly bent. Return to starting position. Alternate sides, doing 5 slides on each side, working up to 10. Do these first three exercises together and in order for the next two weeks, then add move 4.

Benefits: Strengthens the transverse and lower back, supporting your core.

### *4. Towel Pulse*
Lie on your back, knees bent. Place a towel across your upper shins and grasp each end. Pull the ends of the towel and squeeze thighs together. Inhale, then exhale as you draw your abs in and lift your shoulders off the floor. Hold, and contract and release your ab muscles 10 to 12 times, working up to 20. Do moves 1–4 in order for two weeks.

Benefits: Strengthens the transverse.

### *5. Single-Leg Stretch with Towel*
Add this move at 12 to 14 weeks postpartum, doing moves 1–5 in order. Lie on your back with your knees above your hips and your shins parallel to the floor. Place a small towel on top of your thighs, hold on to the ends and push against your thighs to create resistance. Lift your head and shoulders and extend your left leg out as you exhale. Switch legs and repeat, alternating legs for 5 reps and working up to 10.

Benefits: Strengthens the transverse, giving you a stronger, sleeker-looking torso.

**CLEANING WITH KIDS IN THE HOUSE IS LIKE BRUSHING YOUR TEETH WITH OREOS.**

# CHAPTER 4
## *Feet Growth*

WHEN YOU HAVE FOUGHT SO HARD TO GET BACK ON YOUR FEET AND THEN YOU REALIZE YOUR SHOES DON'T FIT ANYMORE.

I remember it like it was yesterday. I had been home for the last two months in grip socks and sweats and was finally going out for a night on the town. I had secured a baby sitter, managed to fit into one of my favorite dresses, and made reservations at my favorite restaurant. All that was missing was a fabulous pair of shoes to make my outfit pop and I knew what pair to put on. My overly expensive Hermes booties. These shoes cost so much that when I bought them, I had to pray and ask for forgiveness for spending so much money for them. I hadn't worn them since becoming pregnant and couldn't wait to put them on.

I pulled the box from the top of the closet, sat on the bed, crossed my right leg over my left and began to get my life all the way together. For some reason, I couldn't get them on. I looked inside the shoe thinking I had left the tissue inside, but there wasn't any. I wiggled and wiggled and after struggling for a few minutes, finally got them on. I stood up and the shoe was so tight on my foot that it was turning red. I was in denial for a few and then finally realized my foot had grown . . . blasphemy!

Feet can grow for a few reasons. The foot is made up of 26 bones and more than 30 joints that are held together by a network of ligaments. During pregnancy, there's a relaxation, or loosening, of the ligaments throughout your whole body due to hormones. It's your body's way of preparing the pelvic joints for childbirth, and your fluctuating hormonal levels are believed to be what causes it.

Researchers found that pregnancy changes the height of the foot's arch. This especially can happen during your first pregnancy. The result is that the foot becomes longer and flatter due to the loss of arch height. Researchers also concluded that this may be the cause of musculoskeletal disorders that many women start to experience with age. However, further research is necessary to determine the link between these and pregnancy, as well as establishing preventive measures.

Obviously, the weight gain during pregnancy can have an impact on the whole body, including the feet. It is important for pregnant women to

# FEET GROWTH

learn about normal weight gain while pregnant. Gaining too much weight can happen due to an unhealthy diet combined with pregnancy hormones. It can also put you and your baby at risk.

If your feet do grow, the good news is that it won't hurt. The only reasons you'd have pain would be if you kept wearing shoes that were too small or if you had another foot problem caused by altered joint function. You'll probably have to go up a half to a whole shoe size. I know, you don't want to give up those cute old Louboutin's, blasphemy! It's important to wear a shoe that fits you well (even after pregnancy) to prevent foot problems. Do what I did and use this as a great excuse to do some shoe shopping.

The good news is that even if your feet grow, they will most likely only grow during your first pregnancy. Also, don't expect to end up with a huge foot. Researchers reported that for most women, the increase was less than one foot size. The bad news is that you will probably remain with a bigger foot size if you experience growing feet during pregnancy.

**If you're freaked out about growing out of your favorite shoes, the good news is that there are a few ways you can reduce your chances that your feet will get bigger:**

1. Wear supportive shoes. Be sure you have shoes that support your arches (think sneakers, not floppy ballet flats) and shoes that don't squeeze or pinch anywhere (stay away from those pointy-toe numbers that don't give you any wiggle room).
2. Try compression socks or stockings. These can help control lower-extremity swelling.
3. Avoid excessive weight gain. Do your best to stay within the recommended weight gain range for your body type to avoid putting unnecessary pressure on your feet.

4. Try supportive insoles. These can be particularly effective if you already have low arches ("flat feet"). Ask your doctor or physical therapist if they might be right for you.

5. Avoid standing for prolonged time periods. If you have a job where you have to stand all day, talk to your employer about possible solutions. Standing also increases other health risks during pregnancy, such as varicose veins or back pain.

6. Take daily walks to help your body cope during pregnancy. Light exercise is also recommended, especially swimming.

7. If you experience swollen feet, talk to your doctor about creams that improve blood circulation during pregnancy. You can also keep your legs elevated using pillows at least one hour a day.

ONE OF MY FRIENDS IS PREGNANT.
AND I'M REALLY EXCITED.
NOT FOR THE BABY, BUT BECAUSE SHE'S
ONE OF MY SKINNIEST FRIENDS.

# CHAPTER 5
## *Skin Change*

EVERY TIME I LOOK IN THE MIRROR,
I HAVE TO LOOK AT MY ID TO MAKE SURE IT'S REALLY ME.

## THANKS FOR TELLING ME

It doesn't matter what your complexion is, if you've had a baby, chances are high you will experience some type of change in your skin's appearance. Some women develop what's called the "mask of pregnancy." That tan-colored area around your eyes will start to fade. Women who suffered from severe acne during pregnancy should see their skin start to clear up. However, other women will begin to experience a red rash around their mouth and chin or suffer from extremely dry skin. Both of these conditions should be gone within weeks.

Just like the rest of your body, your complexion can take a long time to get back to normal (whatever that was for you) after you've delivered. Postpartum skin can also be a result of the way you perceive yourself after delivery. When you're pregnant, the body produces a lot of progesterone, which can enhance your mood. A couple of months after delivery, the level of estrogen will become normal, almost at the same time that you begin to get your periods. After this, your skin will get back its luster and become supple and soft again.

Another reason for postpartum skin is that when you're pregnant, the high level of estrogen and progesterone causes the kidneys to retain water and salt. Because of this, your skin will retain fluids easily and so it will be soft and supple. After the delivery, there is a sharp drop in the level of hormones, and this leads to loss of water and salt. This causes the skin to look less plump. But after the delivery, the level of progesterone drops and you might feel a little low and may not feel happy. That rosy mom-to-be glow (caused by estrogen-fueled blood flow to your skin) may be gone, possibly replaced by postpartum acne, due again to hormonal swings (plus stress, sleep deprivation and about zero time for skin care).

And what about those dark splotches on your forehead, upper lip and cheeks, which have yet to fade? For most women, they will. Those patches (known as melasma, or the mask of pregnancy) are caused by an increase in the production of melanin, a skin pigment, during pregnancy. The good news is your body will eventually stop making so much melanin (though

# SKIN CHANGE

that might not happen until after you wean) and then those darned splotches should start to fade.

To help this process along, stay out of the sun as much as possible and wear a broad-spectrum sunscreen (that blocks both UVA and UVB rays) with an SPF of at least 30. Use it every day, rain or shine. (Another option: a moisturizer or foundation with sun block in it.) This advice holds true even after your splotches have faded, since dark spots are more likely to return once you've had them. Even more important: Regular use of sunscreen protects against skin cancer (and wrinkles!). If you're back on the pill, ask your practitioner about switching to an estrogen-free variety (like the progestin-only "mini pill" or a progesterone injection), since estrogen can sometimes make melasma worse.

Be sure to cleanse your skin gently twice a day to help prevent blemishes. If you do break out, try a product with benzoyl peroxide or glycolic acid (both are fine for nursing mothers) but skip salicylic-acid-based formulas until you've weaned, just to be on the safe side. Your complexion will also benefit from oil-free (non-pore-clogging) cosmetics, and a diet that contains lots of fruits and vegetables, vitamin B2, and plenty of water. Exercise and eat right to help your skin regain its tone and moisturize regularly.

**Tips for skin during postpartum:**

1. You might need to use a thick body lotion or moisturizer to keep your skin soft and supple. Apply the cream twice a day and massage it into your skin. Alternatively, you can even try olive oil or almond oil.

2. Apply the lotion or oil after a bath, when your skin is moist and the cream is absorbed into the skin easily.

3. Avoid using strong soaps as these can strip the moisture from your skin. Use mild, herbal soaps instead.

**4.** The humidity levels in your house should be high, so do remember to turn on the humidifier when you switch on the central heating. Alternatively, place a bowl of water in the room to keep the room humidified.

If you still suffer from postpartum skin rash or postpartum itchy skin, visit a dermatologist. The thing to keep in mind is your baby thinks you're beautiful—stretch marks, freckles and all!

MAKING THE DECISION TO HAVE A CHILD—IT'S MOMENTOUS. IT IS TO DECIDE FOREVER TO HAVE YOUR HEART GO WALKING AROUND OUTSIDE YOUR BODY.

# CHAPTER 6
## *Postpartum Depression*

JUST ALL LOVE AND UNDERSTANDING.

You've probably heard of the "baby blues." That's because it's quite common for new mothers to feel a little sad, worried, or fatigued. As many as 80 percent of mothers have these feelings for a week or two following childbirth. It's completely normal and usually fades in a few weeks. While some of the symptoms sound the same, postpartum depression is different from the baby blues.

Postpartum depression is a lot more powerful and lasts longer. It follows about 15 percent of births, in first-time moms and those who've given birth before. It can cause severe mood swings, exhaustion, and a sense of hopelessness. The intensity of those feelings can make it difficult to care for your baby or yourself. Postpartum depression shouldn't be taken lightly. It's a serious disorder, but it can be overcome through treatment.

Whether a first child or a fifth, postpartum depression can require some patience and understanding from anywhere it can be found. As a new mom, you face a lot of challenges getting used to life with a newborn. You're also probably dealing with lack of sleep, new responsibilities, or even breast pain if you're nursing.

In recent years as postpartum depression has become more commonly known and researched, there have been those who have become rather famous for their postpartum depression quotes. Postpartum depression is a very real mental health issue that has only recently been drawn into the limelight by some horrific events, as well as some open admissions from famous people who may have personal experience with this form of depression.

Postpartum depression is the type of depression you may get after you have a baby. It can start any time during your baby's first year, but it's most common for you to start to feel its effects during the first 3 weeks after birth. It doesn't just affect first-time moms. You can get it even if you didn't have it when your other children were born. There are many causes, including hormones. Your hormone levels rise when you're pregnant. After your baby is born, they drop suddenly. This quick change can trigger depression in some women.

# POSTPARTUM DEPRESSION

**Common symptoms:**

1. You feel sad or cry a lot, even when you don't know why.
2. You're exhausted, but you can't sleep.
3. You sleep too much.
4. You can't stop eating, or you aren't interested in food at all.
5. You have various unexplained aches, pains, or illnesses.
6. You don't know why you're irritable, anxious, or angry.
7. Your moods change suddenly and without warning.
8. You feel out of control.
9. You have difficulty remembering things.
10. You can't concentrate or make simple decisions.
11. You have no interest in things you used to enjoy.
12. You feel disconnected from your baby and wonder why you're not filled with joy like you thought you'd be.
13. Everything feels overwhelming and hopeless.
14. You feel worthless and guilty about your feelings.
15. You feel like you can't open up to anyone because they'll think you're a bad mother or take your baby, so you withdraw.
16. You want to escape from everyone and everything.
17. You have intrusive thoughts about harming yourself or your baby.

**Physical factors:**
Some other physical factors may include:

1. Low thyroid hormone levels
2. Sleep deprivation
3. Inadequate diet

4. Underlying medical conditions
5. Drug and alcohol misuse

**Emotional factors:**
1. Recent divorce or death of a loved one
2. You or your child having serious health problems
3. Social isolation
4. Financial burdens
5. Lack of support

You may be more likely to develop postpartum depression if you've had a mood disorder in the past or if mood disorders run in your family. Talking to a psychologist or therapist can also be a great help. You can learn ways to recognize when you're having negative thoughts, so you know how to deal with them better. You may even discuss past relationships or stresses and learn how to work through those, so they don't affect your life now.

Only a doctor can diagnose you with postpartum depression. But if you think you have it, make an appointment right away. If it's postpartum depression, there are treatments that will get you back to feeling like yourself again. Your doctor might decide that prescribing you antidepressants will help. These drugs help balance certain brain chemicals linked to depression. Most are safe to take while you breastfeed. Just be sure to let your doctor know if you're nursing.

The exact cause of postpartum depression isn't clear, but there are some factors that may contribute to postpartum depression. Postpartum depression may be triggered by a combination of physical changes and emotional stressors.

You might feel more comfortable reaching out to others who've been through the same thing. They understand what you're feeling and can offer nonjudgmental support. Consider joining a group for new mothers. Some of them may also be living with depression, anxiety, or postpartum depression.

## POSTPARTUM DEPRESSION

**These organizations can help guide you to the appropriate resources:**

Postpartum Depression Support Groups in the U.S. and Canada: This is a comprehensive list of support groups around the United States (by state) and Canada.

Postpartum Education for Parents at 805-564-3888: Trained volunteers answer the "warmline" 24/7 to provide support.

Postpartum Progress: This organization has information and support for pregnant women and new moms who have postpartum depression and anxiety.

Postpartum Support International at 800-944-4PPD (800-944-4773): This resource offers education, online support, and information about local resources.

If you don't like one support system, it's okay to try another. Keep trying until you find the help you need.

A COUPLE OF HOURS INTO A VISIT WITH MY MOTHER, SHE NOTICED I HADN'T LIT UP A CIGARETTE ONCE. "ARE YOU TRYING TO KICK THE HABIT?"

"NO," I REPLIED, "I'VE GOT A COLD AND I DON'T SMOKE WHEN I'M NOT FEELING WELL."

"YOU KNOW," SHE OBSERVED, "YOU'D PROBABLY LIVE LONGER IF YOU WERE SICK MORE OFTEN."

# CHAPTER 7
## *Postpartum Bleeding*

I'VE LOST SO MUCH BLOOD THAT THERE'S NO WAY I'M STILL ALIVE.

I anticipated bleeding heavily for weeks on end and stocked up on one million pads, not to mention the duffle bag of pads the hospital sent me home with. But I was surprised by what happened. Sure, the first day or two bleeding was heavy, but things quickly lightened up, even during the first week. Not having a period was fun while it lasted, but eventually that monthly visitor returned. Never has there been a more dreaded return than that of the menstrual cycle after a nine month break from pad changing and aspirin popping. Sure, you know Aunt Flo's going to come back eventually, but what you may not be prepared for are the weird things about your first postpartum period that every woman goes through.

Because having a baby can change more than just the number of people in your family—giving birth can alter the way your period comes back, especially the first time around. Not knowing when or where that first period will strike can be a bit nerve wrecking. When I felt the first niggling of cramps, I stuffed my diaper bag with pads and aspirin so when Aunt Flo showed up, I was more than prepared.

From stressing over your supply of feminine hygiene products to wondering where in the world all the extra blood is coming from, there is really no way to prepare yourself for what will happen. Since your body and hormones changed while you were pregnant, and continue to heal and change again in the postpartum phase, it takes a little bit of time for everything to return to proper working order. Meaning the first cycle you have after delivering your little one could be full of surprises. But you're not alone—women everywhere experience these weird postpartum period occurrences.

**Some things that may occur:**

### 1. Blood Clots
First you may notice blood clots once your period returns after giving birth. But no need to panic, it's probably just clearing things out after all these months with no menstruation.

# POSTPARTUM BLEEDING

*2. Pain*
Although pregnancy isn't always a walk in the park, having a break from your monthly visitor is a nice perk. If you're like me, the first time your period returns, you're a little bit in denial. "Was it really this bad before?" you may wonder. Your minds forget how bad it all can be after months of freedom from pads. For some, the return of the period can be rather hellish, but some women may find a pleasant change of events has occurred.

*3. You May Have A Different Flow*
Just when you thought you knew what Aunt Flo was up to, your period can return either lighter or heavier than before you became pregnant.

*4. You Soak Through*
Make sure you have plenty of back-up packed in your bag when you leave the house, because heavier periods and blood clots could mean you soak through your feminine hygiene products faster than you used to. Staying stocked will keep you from a code red while out and about.

*5. You May See Something Else in There*
If you notice something with a creamy white color mixed in with period blood, there's an explanation for that. Lochia is a type of vaginal discharge which is common after pregnancy, as Healthline explained. Depending on how soon after delivery you start your period, you may see some lochia appear.

*6. You May Notice It Affects Your Breastmilk*
For breastfeeding mamas, changes in breastmilk can accompany that first period. Although it's usually temporary, the reboot of your period can cause your supply to dip, as well as changes to the taste of your breastmilk.

### *7. You May Feel Bummed Out*

I'm not going to lie, when my period came back, it really bummed me out. Not just for the obvious reasons (it's annoying, uncomfortable, etc.), but because it represented the end of a special phase. It felt symbolic, like life was moving on and those special months of pregnancy and newborn bliss were over. Don't be surprised if some unexpected emotions pop-up along with the return of your cycle.

One of the things about postpartum that surprised me was how quickly my bleeding tapered down to light bleeding and then spotting. (Caesarean mothers often have even less bleeding than anticipated too.)

In the first couple of days, bleeding can be heavy. Adult diapers are the way to go! There's no worry of leakage with the adult diaper. It's so easy! I'm a fan of easy when it comes to postpartum. After about 3–7 days, adult diapers become overkill because bleeding has slowed down considerably. I love the "purple pads" for a heavier flow. If conventional pads aren't for you, but cloth pads don't spark joy either, you may be interested in a more natural postpartum or "maternity" pad.

WHILE DOING RENOVATIONS IN OUR HOUSE, ONE OF THE WORKMEN PAUSED TO LOOK AT A FLATTERING PHOTO OF ME WEARING MAKEUP AND A FANCY GOWN. I HEARD HIM LET OUT A LOW WHISTLE AND ASK MY SON, JOSHUA, "WHO'S THAT?"
"THAT'S MY MOM," JOSHUA ANSWERED.
"WOW," THE MAN SAID, "MY MOTHER DOESN'T LOOK LIKE THAT."
"YEAH," MY SON SAID, "WELL, NEITHER DOES MINE."

# CHAPTER 8
## *Breast Growth/Lactation*

Some people think having large breasts makes a woman stupid.
Actually, it's quite the opposite: a woman having large breasts makes men stupid.

## THANKS FOR TELLING ME

**D**uring your first week postpartum, whether you're breastfeeding or not, your breast milk will come in and your breasts will engorge—and they may become bigger, tender and hard. A chain reaction begins the moment your body ejects the placenta. You stop making those pregnancy hormones (estrogen and progesterone) and start making prolactin, the magical hormone that throws the dairy barn inside your breasts into full production mode. Some women have even gone up one to two cup sizes after birth. Your spouse may be elated but make sure to tell him those aren't for him.

Postpartum breast changes include enlargement of the breasts themselves, with the nipples and the areola becoming more pronounced. Besides this, the bumps on the areola that produce oils for lubrication also appear larger than before. During the first few days of breastfeeding, the nipples will tend to feel tender and sore. Postpartum breast pain is caused by the various hormonal changes that take place after you have given birth to your child.

One of the best ways of helping yourself to cope with postpartum breast tenderness is to wear a comfortable bra that gives your breasts the support they require. A cold compress, given by wrapping a packet of ice in a towel and placing the same over the breasts is known to be beneficial in reducing tenderness and pain. Dietary patterns are an important means of helping your body to cope and adapt to various situations, postpartum breast tenderness included. It is, therefore, advisable that you add a lot of fiber to your dietary plan, through the inclusion of fruits and vegetables. Exercise helps to remove excess fluids from the body and is beneficial in reducing the strain of heavy breasts.

During the first two or three days after birth, the breasts tends to secrete a yellow colored fluid, known as colostrum, which is rich in its content of antibodies. Postpartum breasts tend to fill up with milk to feed and nurse the newborn baby, making them feel heavy and extremely sensitive.

Whether you are feeding your baby at the breast or with a bottle, your

## BREAST GROWTH/LACTATION

body will naturally produce milk. As your milk supply increases, your breasts may become very tender and/or swollen. This is called engorgement and begins on the second or third day after your baby's birth. It will last about 24 to 48 hours.

If you are breastfeeding, postpartum breast engorgement should diminish within two to three days. After that, it'll take a few weeks for you and your baby to work out a mutual feeding schedule that satisfies his often unpredictable hunger and your breasts' ability to match it. (That tingling sensation tells you it's baby's feeding time!) If you're not nursing, engorgement should subside within a few days.

Luckily, there are some things you can do for relief.

**If you're nursing:**

1. Try a warm compress before nursing and a cold compress afterwards.

2. Yes, it'll look strange (almost as strange as it sounds), but placing chilled cabbage leaves on each breast (make an opening for your nipple first) will prove surprisingly soothing. Or try some cooling bra inserts (they're available in maternity or baby-supply stores).

3. Use your hand or a pump to express a little milk and relieve a bit of pressure. Don't express too much, though, because that will only make matters worse. (The more you express, the more milk is made—and if it's more than baby's ready to take, you'll wear the rest in engorgement.)

4. Massage your breasts gently while nursing to help get the milk flowing.

5. Alter the position of your baby (try the cradle hold one time, the football hold at the next feeding) to ensure all milk ducts are being emptied.

6. Make sure your bra fits well—not too tight, but snug and supportive.
7. Most important: Feed your baby frequently.
8. For severe pain, consider taking acetaminophen (take it after a feeding) or ask your practitioner for another mild pain reliever.

**If you're not nursing:**
(In order to minimize pain and tenderness and discourage future milk production:)

1. Wear a supportive bra.
2. Avoid any kind of nipple stimulation or milk expression.
3. Use ice packs to help soothe discomfort.

Your breasts will probably become flushed, swollen, sore, and engorged with milk for a day or two after the birth. Once this swelling goes down, in about three to four days (or until you stop breastfeeding), your breasts will probably begin to sag as a result of the stretched skin.

You may also experience milk leakage for several weeks, even if you don't breastfeed.

**If your breasts become engorged when breastfeeding:**

1. Wear a bra with good support 24 hours a day.
2. Take a warm shower or apply a warm face cloth to your breasts. The heat may help milk flow.
3. Pump or hand express milk before nursing to soften the breast if your baby is having trouble latching on because your breasts are engorged.
4. Apply a cold compress after feeding. It may help relieve swelling.
5. Take Tylenol or Motrin for discomfort.

## BREAST GROWTH/LACTATION

6. Nurse your baby frequently to help your milk supply and reduce engorgement.

**If your breasts become engorged when bottle feeding:**

1. Wear a bra with good support 24 hours a day.
2. Avoid handling your breasts.
3. Do not pump or hand express milk. This will only increase the engorgement.
4. Take Tylenol or Motrin for discomfort.

In order to avoid the irritation caused by leaky postpartum breasts, it is advisable that absorbent pads be used. Similar to diapers, they should be thrown out after having been used to soak up excess colostrum that is likely to cause irritation and itchiness.

"WHEN YOUR MOTHER ASKS, 'DO YOU WANT A PIECE OF ADVICE?' IT IS A MERE FORMALITY. IT DOESN'T MATTER IF YOU ANSWER YES OR NO. YOU'RE GOING TO GET IT ANYWAY."

# CHAPTER 9
## *Breastfeeding*

A BULLY ONCE CALLED ME A GRACELESS COW
WHEN I WAS IN HIGH SCHOOL.
BOY WAS SHE WRONG, I'M NOT GRACELESS.

## THANKS FOR TELLING ME

**D**eciding between breastfeeding or bottle-feeding is a personal decision many new parents face when they are about to bring new life into the world. It is one of the first significant parenting decisions a new mom will make and knowing all the facts about both options can greatly help with making this important choice.

The majority of mothers, like myself, intended to breastfeed at birth. Many factors can disrupt this intent. Unfortunately, information about breastfeeding is rarely provided by the obstetricians during prenatal visits and some health professionals incorrectly believe that commercially prepared formula is nutritionally equivalent to breast milk. Many hospitals have instituted practices that encourage breastfeeding, however a 2012 study in the U.S. found that 24% of maternity services were still providing supplements of commercial infant formula as a general practice in the first 48 hours after birth.

Colostrum is the "first milk" that a breastfeeding mother produces in the weeks before delivery and in the early days of breastfeeding. It is just waiting for your baby to be born. This special milk is low in fat and high in carbohydrates, protein, and antibodies; it is also extremely easy to digest. Although the amount of colostrum is low, it is high in concentrated nutrition. It is the perfect first food!

If you worry that you have no milk the first few days after delivery, remember that a little bit of colostrum goes a long way. Put your baby to breast often for him to "sip" on colostrum. This helps bring in your "second milk," the mature milk, sooner.

Colostrum has a laxative effect on your baby, helping him pass meconium which aids in the first bowel movements and helps prevent jaundice.

Colostrum is often called "white blood" because it provides large amounts of living cells (lymphocytes and macrophages, similar to those in blood) which will defend your baby against infections and illnesses.

Colostrum has an especially important role in protecting your baby's gastrointestinal tract. A newborn's intestines are very permeable (leaky). Colostrum seals the microscopic holes by "painting" the gastrointestinal tract with a barrier which prevents most foreign proteins (from food the mother has eaten or from infant formula) from penetrating the gut and possibly sensitizing your baby to an allergy.

Colostrum is considered your baby's first immunization because it contains large quantities of an antibody called secretory immunoglobulin A (sIgA).

As breastmilk changes from colostrum to mature milk, the concentration of immune factors and antibodies decreases but the volume of breastmilk greatly increases. Therefore, the amount of infection fighters your baby receives remains constant throughout breastfeeding.

Both breastfeeding and bottle-feeding have positive and negative aspects, especially with parents 'mommy-shaming' mothers who choose bottle-fed formula over breast milk. There is no right or wrong choice, just the healthiest choice for both mother and child!

Infants should be breastfed exclusively for the first four to six months of their life, and a combination of breastfeeding with solid foods until the age of one. Breastfeeding is highly beneficial for both the mother and baby's health, as there are numerous benefits associated with breastmilk and the physical act of breastfeeding itself. One of the primary benefits is it allows mother and child to bond emotionally due to the intimate act of nourishing the child through their body, similar to when the infant was in utero.

**Breastfeeding has so many benefits for your baby:**

1. It supplies all the necessary nutrients in the proper proportions.
2. It protects against allergies, sickness, and obesity.
3. It protects against diseases, like diabetes and cancer.
4. It protects against infections, like ear infections.
5. It is easily digested—no constipation, diarrhea or upset stomach.

6. Babies have healthier weights as they grow.
7. Breastfed babies score higher on IQ tests.

The milk changes in volume and composition according to the time of day, nursing frequency, and age of baby to promote healthy growth. Breast milk is the perfect food for your baby.

**Mothers who breastfeed:**

1. Have a reduced risk of Type 2 Diabetes and certain cancers such as breast cancer.
2. May find it easier to return to what they weighed before they got pregnant.
3. Strengthen the bond with their children.

Immediately after birth, your baby is eager, alert and ready to breastfeed. Place your baby skin-to-skin immediately after birth and as often as possible during the first days of life. This will help your baby adjust to life outside of your body and to breastfeed better. Full-term infants display many different suckling behaviors or feeding cues, such as bringing their hands to their mouth, rooting, suckling, licking and nuzzling the nipple (a normal behavior). Your baby's suckling reflex is greatest from 45 minutes to 2 hours after birth. The first several feedings have a lasting effect and are a positive and satisfying experience for you and your baby.

Your baby's initial alertness and eagerness is followed by an increasingly deeper sleep. About 20–24 hours of age, your baby will be awake more often and more interested in nursing. When awake, your baby may want to feed often and alternate between light sleep and quiet wakefulness. Your baby may nurse several times close together (cluster feedings) and sleep several hours without nursing. Normal, full-term, healthy newborns may breastfeed every hour or several times in one hour, usually

## BREASTFEEDING

in the evening, late night or early morning hours. Responding to your baby's needs for cluster feedings should help your baby feel satisfied.

A caesarean birth does not directly affect the breastfeeding process. However, discomfort, fatigue and the medications used in surgery may present more of a challenge when you begin breastfeeding. Nurse your baby as soon after delivery as possible (8 to 12 times per 24-hour period). Once you begin regular feedings, your milk supply will increase the first few days of breastfeeding.

Research shows that the critical days for breastfeeding success are the first six to seven days after delivery, and later near the baby's sixth week. It is important to get the help you need during these times. Fatigue may play a large role in any doubts about continuing breastfeeding. If possible, get help with the household chores and infant care, allowing time for rest and comfort. Do not hesitate to accept help when offered. Simplify the chores as much as possible, such as using paper plates/cups or a grocery delivery service.

Create a peaceful comfortable "nursing station" and allow yourself to relax.

Find a comfortable position, such as in a chair with ample room on the sides and back for pillows to support your baby and your arms. Sitting with your legs up on a bed or using a footstool when in a chair will help you feel more comfortable.

Unwrap your baby and check if his/her diaper needs to be changed. This will help arouse and stimulate your baby to nurse, especially if your baby is sleepy. If your baby is awake and ready to nurse, wait until after your baby finishes nursing on the first breast to change your baby's diapers.

After the initial quiet alert state following birth, it is normal for babies to be sleepy for the next 24 hours. Breastfeed 8 to 12 times per 24-hour period.

## Common breastfeeding issues:

### *1. Latching pain*
It's normal for your nipples to feel sore when you first start to breastfeed, especially if you're a first-timer. But if baby has latched and the pain lasts longer than a minute into your feeding session, check the positioning.

Solution: Try to achieve an asymmetrical latch where baby's mouth covers more of the areola below the nipple rather than above. To reposition him, place your index finger inside baby's mouth to take him off your breast. Tickle his chin or wait until he yawns so his mouth is wide open and seize your opportunity. Sandwich the breast to shape it to the baby's mouth. When he is correctly positioned, his chin and nose touch your breast, his lips splay out and you can't see your nipple or part of the lower areola.

If baby's position is correct and latching on still hurts, your nipples may be dry. Make sure to wear loose clothing and avoid washing with soap. Lanolin-based creams are good for applying between feedings.

### *2. Cracked nipples*
Cracked nipples can be the result of many different things: thrush (see #6), dry skin, pumping improperly, or most likely, latching problems. During the first week of breastfeeding, you may have bloody discharge when your baby is just learning to latch or you are just beginning to pump. A little blood, while kind of gross, won't harm baby.

Solution: Check baby's positioning—the bottom part of your areola underneath your nipple should be in baby's mouth. Also, try breastfeeding more frequently, and at shorter intervals. The less hungry baby is, the softer his sucking will be.

As tempting as it is to treat your cracked nipples with anything you can find in your medicine cabinet, soaps, alcohol, lotions, and perfumes are no good—clean water is all you need to wash with. Try letting some milk stay on your nipples to air dry after feeding (the milk actually helps heal them). You can also try taking a mild painkiller like acetaminophen or ibuprofen 30 minutes before nursing. If all this fails, try an over-the-counter lanolin cream specially made for nursing mothers and use plastic hard breast shells inside your bra.

### *3. Clogged/plugged ducts*

Ducts clog because your milk isn't draining completely. You may notice a hard lump on your breast or soreness to the touch and even some redness. If you start feeling feverish and achy, that's a sign of infection and you should see your doctor. Most importantly, try not to have long stretches in between feedings—milk needs to be expressed often. A nursing bra that is too tight can also cause clogged ducts. Stress (something all new mommies have an overabundance of) can also affect your milk flow.

Solution: Do your best to get adequate rest (you should recruit your partner to pick up some slack when possible). Also, try applying warm compresses to your breasts and massage them to stimulate milk movement. Clogged ducts are not harmful to your baby because breastmilk has natural antibiotics. That said, there's no reason why you have to suffer. Breastfeeding should be enjoyable for mom and baby.

### *4. Engorgement/high milk supply*

Engorgement makes it difficult for baby to latch on to the breast because it's hard and un-conforming to his mouth.

Solution: Try hand-expressing a little before feeding to get the milk flowing and soften the breast, making it easier for baby to latch and access milk. Of course, the more you nurse, the less likely your breasts are to get engorged.

### 5. Mastitis

Mastitis is a bacterial infection in your breasts marked by flu-like symptoms such as fever and pain in your breasts. It's common within the first few weeks after birth (though it can also happen during weaning) and is caused by cracked skin, clogged milk ducts, or engorgement.

Solution: The only sufficient way to treat the infection is with antibiotics, hot compresses, and most importantly, frequent emptying. Use hands-on pumping, making sure the red firm areas of the breast and the periphery are softened. It's safe and actually recommended that you continue breastfeeding when you have mastitis.

### 6. Thrush

Thrush is a yeast infection in your baby's mouth, which can also spread to your breasts. It causes incessant itchiness, soreness, and sometimes a rash.

Solution: Your doctor will need to give you antifungal medication to put on your nipple and in baby's mouth—if you're not both treated at the same time, you can give each other the fungi and prolong healing.

### 7. Low milk supply

Breastfeeding is a supply-and-demand process. If your doctor is concerned about baby's weight gain, and he is being plotted on the World Health Organization curves designed for breastfeeding babies, this may be the problem.

Solution: Frequent nursing and hands-on pumping during the day can help increase milk supply. Surprisingly, forcing fluids and eating more calories or different foods hasn't been shown to increase milk production.

### *8. Baby sleeping at breast*

Baby is sleepy in the first couple of months after birth (hey, he's been through a lot) so falling asleep while nursing is common. All that bonding makes baby relaxed!

Solution: Milk flow is fastest after your first let-down, so if you want to increase efficiency, start off at the fuller breast, then switch to the other breast sooner, rather than later. When you notice baby's sucking slowing down and his eyes closing, remove him from your breast and try to stimulate him by burping, tickling his feet, or gently talking to him while rubbing his back, and then switch breasts. As baby gets older, he'll be able to stay awake longer, so don't fret.

### *9. Inverted/flat nipples*

You can tell if you have flat or inverted nipples by doing a simple squeeze test: Gently grab your areola with your thumb and index finger—if your nipple retracts rather than protrudes, you've got a problem, Houston. Not really. But breastfeeding will be more challenging.

Solution: Use a pump to get the milk flowing before placing baby at your nipple and use breast shells between feeds. Once you feel like your milk supply is adequate, try using nipple shields if baby still has problems latching.

### *10. Painful/overactive let down*

Your breast is like a machine—when you let down, all the milk-producing engines constrict to move the milk forward and out of your nipple. Sometimes the working of these inner parts can hurt, especially when in overdrive. Some mothers feel a prickly pins-and-needles sensation and others just get an achy feeling.

Solution: If this feeling of pins and needles goes beyond a mere tingling and feels more like a hundred little daggers poking your breasts, you need to check for a breast infection (yeast or bacteria). Sometimes this pain develops when you have an excessive amount of milk. Try feeding baby longer on one particular breast and switching to the other only if you need to. If the result is an infection (fever, aches, and chills may be present), you'll need to get antibiotics from your doctor. No matter how unpleasant it is for you, it's still safe for baby to nurse.

Latching on can be difficult. Just remember, if it hurts then the latch is wrong. If your baby latches onto only your nipple and not the areola, problems may develop, such as sore nipples and a poor milk supply for your baby. You may have to repeat these steps several times before your baby latches-on correctly.

Sit tummy-to-tummy with your baby. Make sure your baby's ear, shoulder and hip are in a straight line and the baby's nose is level with the nipple.

Bring your baby close to your breast. Touch your nipple to your baby's lips. When your baby's mouth opens wide, quickly pull your baby in to latch-on since the mouth will be open for only a few seconds.

**NOTE:** Bring your baby to your breast, rather than bringing your breast to your baby's mouth.

Your baby will be able to breathe even though his/her nose may press into your breast. It is helpful in the first week to continue to support the weight of your breast throughout the nursing session. Support your baby's head at the base of the neck as well.

**Look for the following after your baby is latched-on:**

Your baby's chin should be touching the breast and the baby's mouth should be fully open to take as much areola as possible.

# BREASTFEEDING

Your baby's lips should be turned outward against the breast.

The motion of the suck is along the jaw, not in the cheeks.

Your baby's ears, shoulder and hip should be in a straight line.

Breastfeeding should not hurt. You should feel a strong rhythmic tug on your breast. A little bit of nipple tenderness within the first minute is normal during the learning period. However, sore, reddened, bleeding or cracked nipples are not normal.

**Breastfeeding positions:**

***1. Cradle hold (tummy-to-tummy)***
Sit comfortably. A pillow or footstool may help.

Cradle your baby with your arm, his/her tummy against yours and head resting in the bend of your elbow. Keep your baby's ear, shoulders and hip in a straight line.

Tuck your baby's lower arm under your arm or under your breast with his/her mouth close to your breast.

Support your breast with your free hand; place all of your fingers underneath it, well away from the areola.

Rest your thumb lightly on top of your breast above your areola.

Lift your breast upward and lightly stroke your nipple on your baby's lower lip. As part of the rooting reflex, his/her mouth will open wide. This may take a few minutes to happen.

Pull your baby quickly onto the breast to latch-on when his/her mouth is opened wide, like a big yawn, and the tongue is down. Do not lean over your baby. Instead pull your baby up to your breast.

For laid back breastfeeding, mother relaxes in a reclined position with the baby positioned tummy-to tummy so baby can use his/her instincts to get to the breast. Allow baby's cheek to rest somewhere near the bare breast. Mother can hold breast or not depending on what is comfortable for her. This is a learning process and may take time for baby to latch.

**2. Cross cradle hold (*tummy-to-tummy*)**
Sit comfortably. A pillow or footstool may help.

Cradle your baby with your arm, his/her tummy against yours, and your hand at the base of the head and neck. Keep your baby's ear, shoulders and hip in a straight line.

Tuck your baby's lower arm out of the way, with his/her mouth close to your breast. (You will use opposite hands from the cradle hold.)

Support your breast with your free hand; place all of your fingers underneath it, well away from the areola.

Rest your thumb lightly on top of your breast above your areola.

Lift your breast upward and lightly stroke your nipple on your baby's lower lip. As part of the rooting reflex, his/her mouth will open wide. This may take a few minutes to happen.

Pull your baby quickly onto your breast to latch-on when his/her mouth is opened wide, like a big yawn, and the tongue is down. Do not lean over your baby. Instead pull your baby up to your breast.

# BREASTFEEDING

The cross-cradle hold is good when:

Nursing a newborn infant.

Learning how to position an infant correctly.

### 3. *Football hold*
Position your baby so his/her legs and body are under your arm, with your hand at the base of the head and neck (as if you were holding a football).

Place your fingers below your breast. Allow your baby to latch-on while pulling him/her in close, holding your baby's head with his/her nose and chin touching your breast.

Keep your baby's body flexed at the hip with the legs tucked under your arm.

The football hold is a good position when:

You have had a caesarean birth and want to avoid placing your baby against your abdominal incision.

You need to see better when getting your baby to latch-on.

Your breasts are large.

You are nursing a small baby, especially if premature.

Your baby tends to slide down your areola onto your nipple.

Your baby is fussy, restless and having a hard time latching-on.

Your baby is sleepy. Sitting upright may encourage your baby to remain alert for a longer time.

You have inverted nipples.

**4. *Side-lying position***
First, position yourself and your baby lying down on your sides tummy-to-tummy.

Bend your top leg and position with pillows under your upper knee.

Place your fingers beneath your breast and lift upward, then pull your baby in close as he/she latches-on.

The side-lying position is an especially good choice for breastfeeding when:

You must be flat after a caesarean birth with spinal anesthesia.

You are uncomfortable sitting up (episiotomy or hemorrhoid pain).

You need help from someone else to get your baby latched-on.

You are tired and want to rest.

Be sure to break the suction by slipping your little finger in the corner of your baby's mouth between the gums. Do not remove your baby from your breast until the suction is released, or you may develop sore nipples. The suction is quite strong, and it may require some effort to release your baby's grip.

Not every breastfed baby needs to burp with every feeding. Generally, breastfed babies do not swallow as much air as bottle fed babies do. If your baby has been crying before the feeding, and is pulling on and off the breast, try burping, then try breastfeeding again. Some babies do not burp right away, and you may need to try several positions.

**Helpful positions for burping your baby include:**

1. Propped up with baby's tummy against your shoulder.
2. Lying tummy-down across your lap.
3. Sitting up, leaning forward with your hand on the left side of the baby's body supporting the baby's stomach and neck.

DON'T WORRY, YOU'RE NOT THE FIRST MOM TO THROW A TOWEL OVER THE PEED-ON SHEETS AND GONE BACK TO BED.

# CHAPTER 10
## *Sweating*

I THINK IT RAINED IN MY ROOM LAST NIGHT?

## THANKS FOR TELLING ME

One of the things about postpartum that surprises some new mothers are night sweats. I never experienced nighttime sweats, but generally, I was VERY hot postpartum. At the drop of a hat, I could feel overheated and start sweating. It was so strange! Hello, hormonal rollercoaster. If you're afraid you went directly from pregnancy to menopause, allow me to ease your mind. Waking up with night sweats is a weird postpartum experience, but totally legit. You're just losing all the excess water you've retained during pregnancy or from receiving fluids during delivery.

Night sweats are typically caused by the wonky hormonal changes that are happening. This is because your body needs to get rid of all the extra fluids it accumulated during your pregnancy. Think about it, your body produced a certain combination of hormones to support pregnancy, but now that baby is born, your body needs something completely new—especially if you're breastfeeding.

Many women report waking up in the middle of the night completely soaked in sweat. So much so that it makes sense to change the sheets. These night sweats are totally inconvenient, especially if it chills the body too much, and makes mama super cold. This can make disrobing for breastfeeding a chilly experience! As time goes by, these become less and less and this strange process is only temporary.

Sweating in the night can happen for a number of reasons. Sometimes, waking up warm and sweaty isn't considered "night sweats" at all. Instead, it just means you're too hot or snuggling with too many blankets. Other times, night sweats might be a side effect of a medication or a symptom of a medical issue like anxiety, hyperthyroidism, obstructive sleep apnea, or menopause.

You may also have excess sweating in the days and nights after childbirth. Your hormones are tasked with helping rid your body of excess fluids that supported your body and baby during pregnancy. Along with sweating, you may notice that you're urinating more frequently, which is another way your body flushes out all that extra water weight.

## SWEATING

Night sweating is most common in the days and weeks after birth. It typically doesn't signal any more serious medical issues. If your sweating persists for longer, contact your doctor to rule out infection or other complications.

Waking up drenched may be extremely uncomfortable. There are a few things you can do to feel better when your night sweats are at their worst. First, try to remember that this postpartum symptom is only temporary. Your hormones and fluid levels should regulate on their own soon enough.

**In the meantime:**
Drink plenty of water. All that sweating can leave you dehydrated. It's important to keep up with your fluid intake, especially if you're breastfeeding. You should be using the bathroom frequently, and your urine should be a light or clear color. If your urine is dark, then you're probably not drinking enough water.

Change your pajamas. Even before you start sweating, you can help keep yourself cool by wearing loose, light layers instead of heavy pajamas. Cotton and other natural fibers are better than synthetic fabric at letting your body breathe.

Cool down the room. Whether you turn on the fan or air conditioner, or open a window, lowering the temperature in your bedroom a bit should help ward off some sweating.

Cover your sheets. You may need to change your clothing often, but you can limit sheet changes by covering your sheets with a towel. Worried about your mattress? You can protect it with a rubber sheet underneath your regular bedding.

Consider using powder. If your night sweats are causing skin issues, you can try sprinkling some talc-free powder on your body to prevent rashes.

# THANKS FOR TELLING ME

Contact your doctor if you notice that your night sweats last longer than several weeks after delivery, or if they're accompanied by fever or other symptoms. A fever may be an indication of an infection, so it's important to get checked out.

**Complications after childbirth might include:**
- Wound infection (at caesarean delivery site)
- Blood clots, specifically deep vein thrombophlebitis
- Womb infection (endometritis)
- Breast infection (mastitis)
- Excess bleeding
- Postpartum depression

**Be sure to call your doctor if you experience any of the following symptoms:**
- Fever over 100.4°F
- Unusual or foul vaginal discharge
- Large clots or bright red bleeding more than three days after delivery
- Pain or burning with urination
- Pain, redness, or drainage at the incision or stitches site
- Warm, red areas on your breasts
- Severe cramping
- Trouble breathing, dizziness, or fainting
- Feeling particularly depressed or anxious

You should also keep your 6-week appointment after delivery so your doctor can ensure you're healing properly. This appointment is also a great time to discuss birth control, postpartum depression, or any other concerns you may have.

## SWEATING

Waking up in the night to feed, change, and soothe your newborn may feel difficult if you are also sweating through your clothing. If you believe your night sweats are unusually heavy or have lasted a long time, you may want to ask your doctor:

Could any of my medications be causing night sweats? You don't need to suffer alone. That being said, your body is likely just continuing its tremendous transition from pregnancy to postpartum. Take care of yourself and your growing baby. You should be back to feeling more like yourself soon.

**PEOPLE WHO SAY "I SLEPT LIKE A BABY" USUALLY DON'T HAVE ONE.**

# CHAPTER 11
## *Sleep*

After giving birth, I realized there is no sunrise so beautiful that I need to wake up to see it. I would prefer to see the inside of my eyelids.

**B**ecoming a parent only further stretches our already-too-thin sleep allotments. Newborn babies wake frequently to feed or for comfort during the night. We try to "sleep when the baby sleeps" and piece it together to come up with a reasonable amount, but it often doesn't feel sufficient. And now more than ever, new parents are really isolated as they make this transition. They don't have much in the way of backup resources to help with the 24/7 job of caring for a baby.

Sleep deprivation is an inevitable part of having a baby, and surely that's been true throughout the history of our species. But we also live in a culture that seems to take some amount of pride in getting by on little sleep. We think of sleep as time wasted, as lost productivity. We forget—or ignore—the biological necessity of sleep.

I know that you know that sleep deprivation sucks, and I don't mean for this to be a downer. Is there anything we can we do to make things better? I can't claim to have answers, but I'll offer some suggestions:

Cut yourself some slack. This parenting job is hard enough as it is. Doing it on little sleep every day? It's a herculean task, and yet we do it. Sometimes we need to just focus on the basics and have popcorn for dinner.

Prioritize sleep. It's so critical to our health and happiness. The dishes in the sink? They aren't nearly as important.

Give yourself a bedtime. We know our kids don't function well if they're short on sleep. We don't either—we're just a little better at hiding it.

Get help. This is particularly critical for parents of newborns. It may require creative delegation of tasks to friends and family so that you can squeeze in a longer nap or an earlier bedtime. They're happy to help, and you need it. We were never meant to parent alone.

Help your baby develop healthy sleep patterns. And if your older baby is struggling with sleep (and by extension, you are too), know that it is not selfish to make changes that help everyone get the rest they need.

Avoid screen time before bed. It gets in the way of melatonin release, confusing the biological clock trying to keep time in our brains and prepare us for sleep. Yes, your Facebook feed may be your lifeline to the world, but it could also be keeping you up at night.

Be aware of your sleep debt. I think that after a while, we forget how much sleep we're missing. Six hours a night and chronic daytime yawns become our new normal. But knowing that we're behind on sleep, combined with the knowledge of the profound effects of sleep debt on mood and cognition, can give us valuable perspective. Maybe, for example, your partner is being just a little bit of an ass instead of the complete asshole that you perceive. Maybe catching up on sleep will help the day's problems seem a little more manageable.

BEING A MOM MEANS BEING THE FIRST ONE UP IN THE MORNING, THE LAST ONE TO BED AT NIGHT, AND THE ONLY ONE DRINKING DURING CHURCH.

# CHAPTER 12
## *Sex Drive*

I SHOULDN'T BE HAVING THIS MUCH SEX.
I'M MARRIED FOR CRYING OUT LOUD!

It's common to have a low libido in the weeks or even months after having a baby. In the first six weeks after delivery, you're likely to be exhausted, and possibly sore and overwhelmed. Your body needs time to heal. And you're dealing with the 24/7 demands of caring for a newborn.

You're likely to have less natural vaginal lubrication in the first four to six weeks after the birth due to your body's decreasing level of estrogen during this time. If you're breastfeeding your baby, this dryness may continue for as long as you continue to nurse. Or it may return slowly as your nursing sessions become less frequent.

There are plenty of other reasons you may not feel like having sex right now. Adjusting to motherhood may be stressful or emotionally all-consuming. You may feel less attractive or less confident in your changing body at this point. You may fear becoming pregnant again, particularly if you are using a new form of contraception. Or you may be struggling with baby blues or postpartum depression. A number of factors contribute to these feelings.

First, your sex drive has to compete with the overwhelming fatigue that results from taking care of a newborn. New babies are demanding. They require round-the-clock attention and a great deal of physical contact. This can be both physically and emotionally draining. When you finally have a moment to yourself, you may need a break from intense physical attachment, making sex low on your list of priorities.

Second, your body is healing from the ordeal of labor and delivery. Major hormonal shifts are taking place that can make you feel off balance. You may also worry that intercourse will be painful, and for many women, the first sexual encounters after childbirth are uncomfortable. Also, your body is still recovering from giving birth, and you may not feel as attractive as usual. These feelings can have a dramatic impact on your body image and make you feel less sexy and desirable.

Third, you may consciously or subconsciously fear becoming pregnant again. Evolution may help explain this. In nature, mother animals rarely mate when they're busy rearing their young. Their bodies just wouldn't be up to the additional burden of another pregnancy. The same may be true of women.

The good news is that most women report that this decrease in libido is temporary. With time and patience, you and your partner can rebuild a satisfying sexual relationship.

Sexual intimacy needs to be a priority—something that you literally put on the to-do list. You and your partner need to schedule specific times to have sex and be intimate with each other. Make sure there aren't a lot of distractions during this time. The computer and TV should be turned off and cell phones put away.

I know of plenty of husbands who say, "I think my wife is sexy as hell," but their wives are saying, "I've been peed on, pooped on, and I haven't seen the gym in four months. I do not feel sexy." This is where there's a big disconnect.

Moms need to take action to regain their sexual self-esteem. Pick up some new lingerie, buy some new clothes, go for energetic walks. Ask yourself, what is it going to take for me to feel more sexy? A spa day? Getting a manicure? Going to the gym? This isn't something guys can take responsibility for. You need to.

Dads need to do their part as well. A lot of moms end up being the gatekeepers of the baby and manager of all the chores and tasks. If a woman has a ton of chores to do—like getting the laundry done, giving the baby a bath—she's distracted and exhausted.

I suggest men engage in a little "chore play." It's the new foreplay. If Dad really pitches in and gets things done, it's a good way to free up evening time so you can be intimate together.

Remember that sex begets sex. Having sex raises your natural free testosterone level and will help you get back into the swing. Often new moms say they're too tired for sex, and when they have a free moment they just want some sleep. But after they've had sex, they actually feel rejuvenated and wonder why they don't have it more often.

When women are breastfeeding, caressing, and connecting with their baby, it's very intense and emotional. In fact, a lot of new moms say they feel like they're having an affair with their baby. And then you hear men say, "Hey, what about me!"

It's important to realize that if you completely disconnect from your partner because all your physical and emotional attention is sent to your baby, in the end you'll have an unhappy family. So even though your baby is consuming so much of your time and energy—and is completely irresistible—don't forget about Dad.

Couples can engage in nonsexual physical intimacy all the time. Hold hands, cuddle, sit next to each other. And be sexual a minimum of once a week. When you're sexually intimate once a week, you're staying connected and committing to intimacy.

Many caregivers recommend waiting about four weeks after you give birth for sex. It's definitely not safe to have intercourse involving penetration until at least two weeks after delivery. During this time, you're usually still bleeding and at risk for a hemorrhage or uterine infection.

If you have stitches though—either from a c-section, a perineal tear or an episiotomy—it's likely that your caregiver will advise you to wait until after your six-week postpartum visit.

If you're not ready to resume your sex life yet, give yourself a break. You need time to adjust both physically and emotionally to the demands of caring for a baby, and there's no need to rush into having sex until you feel ready. In time, sex can be as satisfying as it was before your baby came along. After you get your caregiver's go-ahead, it's okay to start having sex again as soon as you feel ready and not before.

**GUILT MANAGEMENT CAN BE JUST AS IMPORTANT AS TIME MANAGEMENT FOR MOTHERS.**

# CHAPTER 13
## *Dental*

"Some tortures are physical and some are mental,
but the one that is both is dental."

**P**regnancy can lead to dental problems in some women, including gum disease and increased risk of tooth decay. During pregnancy, your increased hormones can affect your body's response to plaque (the layer of germs on your teeth).

Pregnancy does not automatically damage your teeth. The old wives' tale that warns a woman to expect a lost tooth for every baby is false. If the mother's intake of calcium is inadequate during pregnancy, her bones—not her teeth—will provide the calcium her growing baby needs. This calcium loss is quickly made up after breastfeeding is stopped.

However, the demands of pregnancy can lead to particular dental problems in some women. With proper hygiene at home and professional help from your dentist, your teeth should remain healthy throughout pregnancy.

You are less likely to have dental problems during pregnancy if you already have good oral hygiene habits.

**Suggestions include:**

- Brush your teeth at least twice daily with fluoridated toothpaste.
- Floss between your teeth.
- Visit your dentist regularly.

If you are planning on getting pregnant, but you are also planning on having some elective dental procedures, see your dentist. It is more convenient to have elective procedures done before you conceive. If you require dental treatment during pregnancy, non-urgent procedures are often performed after the first trimester.

Pregnancy may affect your dental care. For example, the dentist may put off taking x-rays until after the birth of your baby. If dental x-rays are unavoidable, the dentist can take precautions to ensure your baby's safety. If your dental condition requires general anesthesia or medications, talk to your dentist, doctor or obstetrician for advice.

# DENTAL

**Causes of dental health problems and common causes of dental health problems during pregnancy can include:**

- Gum problems
- Vomiting
- Retching while brushing teeth
- Cravings for sugary foods

**Gum problems:**
The hormones associated with pregnancy can make some women susceptible to gum problems including:

Gingivitis (gum inflammation)—this is more likely to occur during the second trimester. Symptoms include swelling of the gums and bleeding, particularly during brushing and when flossing between teeth.

Undiagnosed or untreated periodontal disease—pregnancy may worsen this chronic gum infection, which is caused by untreated gingivitis and can lead to tooth loss, pregnancy epulis or pyogenic granuloma—a localized enlargement of the gum, which can bleed easily. This may require additional professional cleaning, and rarely excision.

During pregnancy, the gum problems that occur are not due to increased plaque, but a worsened response to plaque as a result of increased hormone levels.

Tell your dentist about any gum problems that you might have. Switch to a softer toothbrush and brush your teeth regularly, at least twice every day. Use toothpaste that contains fluoride (if you're not already doing so) to help strengthen your teeth against decay.

If you have gum problems during pregnancy, it is important to get your gums checked by a dentist after you have given birth. While most types of gum problems caused by pregnancy hormones resolve after birth, a small number of women may have developed a deeper level of gum disease that will need treatment to resolve.

**Vomiting can damage teeth:**
Pregnancy hormones soften the ring of muscle that keeps food inside the stomach. Gastric reflux (regurgitating food or drink) or the vomiting associated with morning sickness can coat your teeth with strong stomach acids. Repeated reflux and vomiting can damage tooth enamel and increase the risk of decay.

Suggestions Include:

Avoid brushing your teeth immediately after vomiting. While the teeth are covered in stomach acids, the vigorous action of the toothbrush may scratch the tooth enamel.

Rinse your mouth thoroughly with plain tap water.

Follow up with a fluoridated mouthwash.

If you don't have a fluoridated mouthwash, put a dab of fluoridated toothpaste on your finger and smear it over your teeth. Rinse thoroughly with water.

Brush your teeth at least an hour after vomiting.

**Retching while brushing teeth:**
Some pregnant women find that brushing their teeth, particularly the molars, provokes retching. However, you risk tooth decay if you don't brush regularly.

# DENTAL

Suggestions include:

Use a brush with a small head, such as a brush made for toddlers.

Take your time. Slow down your brushing action.

It may help to close your eyes and concentrate on your breathing.

Try other distractions, such as listening to music.

If the taste of the toothpaste seems to provoke your gag reflex, switch to another brand. Alternatively, brush your teeth with water and follow up with a fluoridated mouthwash. Go back to brushing with fluoridated toothpaste as soon as you can.

**Cravings for sugary foods**
Some women experience unusual food cravings (and food avoidance) while they are pregnant. A regular desire for sugary snacks may increase your risk of tooth decay. Try to snack on low-sugar foods instead.

If nothing but sweetness will satisfy your craving, try to sometimes choose healthier options such as fresh fruits. Rinse your mouth with water or an alcohol-free mouth rinse, or brush your teeth after having sugary snacks.

You need to increase your daily amount of calcium during pregnancy. Sufficient calcium will protect your bone mass and meet the nutritional needs of your developing baby.

**Good sources of dietary calcium include products such as:**
- Milk
- Cheese

- Unsweetened yogurt
- Calcium-fortified soymilk

**Increase your vitamin D during pregnancy:**
Vitamin D helps the body to utilize calcium. Good sources include:

- Cheese
- Fortified margarine
- Fatty fish, such as salmon
- Eggs

WE USED TO WANT IT ALL,
NOW WE JUST WANT TO PEE ALONE.

# CHAPTER 14
## *Bladder*

To pee or not to pee, that is the question.

**P**ostpartum urinary incontinence—the involuntary leaking of urine that new moms often experience, usually while laughing, sneezing, coughing, or performing any strenuous activity—is very common after giving birth. About two-thirds of women with "stress incontinence" also experience "urge incontinence," which is caused by an overactive bladder. You get the sudden urge to go, even though your bladder may be nearly empty, and you leak before you can get to the bathroom.

During delivery, the ligaments and muscles that support the bladder and urethra are stretched. In addition, there is a change in some of the enzymes and hormones that make ligaments elastic. Because the muscles and ligaments are weakened, urine may leak out, especially when a woman coughs, laughs, exercises, sneezes, or lifts something.

These are all activities that physically stress the bladder, hence the name stress incontinence. The bladder is like a balloon, with a stubby knob at the end called the urethra. Normally, the bladder relaxes to accommodate urine as it fills. The fuller it gets, the more the sphincter muscle around the urethra squeezes to keep the urine contained.

Women older than 35 and obese women are at greater risk for prenatal leakage of both varieties. After childbirth, the biggest risk factor for stress incontinence is having had a vaginal delivery, especially one involving forceps or other interventions that can injure pelvic nerves and muscles.

**Some treatments for urinary incontinence:**
Though it might be tempting to schedule a C-section to lower your odds of urinary incontinence, experts advise against this. For one thing, susceptibility is to some degree genetic, and a substantial number of women who choose C-sections end up leaking anyway. Research shows that two decades after giving birth, women who delivered via C-section are no better off, leakage-wise, than women who delivered vaginally. "Things tend to equalize due to wear and tear and gravity."

## Kegel exercises

These increase the strength and elasticity of your pelvic floor muscles. Here's a primer: Lie down, knees bent and legs parted. Tighten the muscles around your vagina and urethra as if you're trying to prevent urine or gas from leaking out. Place one hand on your lower abdomen and make sure you're not pushing or contracting your abdominal muscles. (If you're pushing down on your abdominal muscles or squeezing your thighs or buttocks, you're not doing the Kegels correctly.)

While breathing, tighten your vaginal muscles. Think of the pelvic floor as an elevator: Contract muscles in stages, rising to successive levels slowly, in intervals of five to ten seconds. Aim to accomplish sets of ten, three to four times a day, every other day.

If you're leaking while pregnant, Kegel exercises may not be enough to stop the spritz. Experts believe that the weight of the uterus combined with pregnancy hormones make for an overpowering combo. But it still pays to start getting your pelvic-floor muscles in shape. Research suggests that after delivery, Kegel exercises, if done properly, can help minimize both stress and urge incontinence. "You can Kegel immediately, right in your hospital bed," says Missy Lavender, founder of the Women's Health Foundation, a nonprofit group that educates women about pelvic health.

It can take between three to six months, or even longer for some women, to regain complete bladder control. If these treatments don't work, your doctor may conduct further testing to identify the problem. While stress incontinence is the most likely scenario in postpartum women, there are other possible causes, such as nerve damage, loss of muscular support, sphincter muscle problems, or injury to the bladder.

# *References*

Gao C, et al. (2018). Association of vasomotor symptoms and sleep apnea risk in midlife women. DOI:10.1097/GME.0000000000001020

Mayo Clinic Staff. (2018). Night sweats. mayoclinic.org/symptoms/night-sweats/basics/definition/SYM-20050768

Physical changes after delivery. (2016). my.clevelandclinic.org/health/diseases_conditions/hic_Am_I_Pregnant/hic_Labor_and_Delivery/hic_Physical_Changes_After_Delivery

Warning signs of health problems after birth. (2018). marchofdimes.org/pregnancy/warning-signs-after-birth.aspx

Your body after birth: The first 6 weeks. (2018). marchofdimes.org/pregnancy/your-body-after-baby-the-first-6-weeks.aspx

Black R, Morris S, Bryce J. Child Survival I: where and why are 10 million children dying every year? Lancet. 2003, 361:2226-34.

WHO Collaborative Study Team on the Role of Breastfeeding in the Prevention of Infant Mortality. Effect of breastfeeding on infant and childhood mortality due to infectious diseases in less developed countries: a pooled analysis. Lancet. 2000, 355:451-5.

WHO. Global strategy for infant and young child feeding. The optimal duration of exclusive breastfeeding. Geneva: World Health Organization, 2001.

# REFERENCES

WHO. Infant and young child feeding. 2011.www.who.int/nutrition/databases/infantfeeding/countries/en/index.html. Bolling K, et al. Infant feeding survey 2005. London: The Information Centre for Health and Social Care, UK Health Department, 2007.

Adams C. Breastfeeding trends at a community breastfeeding center: an evaluative study. Journal of Obstetric, Gynecologic and Neonatal Nursing. 2001, 30:392-400.

Wagner C. Breastfeeding rates at an urban medical university after initiation of an education program. Southern Medical Journal. 2002, 95:909-13.

Harder T, et al. Duration of breastfeeding and risk of overweight: A meta-analysis. American Journal of Epidemiology. 2005, 162:397-403.

Owen C, et al. Effect of infant feeding on the risk of obesity across the life course: a quantitative review of published literature. Pediatrics. 2005, 115:1367-70.

Horta BL, Victora CG. Long-term effects of breastfeeding: a systematic review. Geneva, Switzerland: World Health Organization, 2013.

Dyson L, McCormick F, Renfrew M. Interventions for promoting the initiation of breastfeeding. Cochrane Database of Systematic Reviews. 2005, 2:CD001688.

Lumbiganon P, et al. Antenatal breastfeeding education for increasing breastfeeding duration. Cochrane Database of Systematic Reviews. 2012, 9:CD006425.

Chapman DJ, et al. Breastfeeding peer counseling: from efficacy through scale-up. Journal of Human Lactation. 2010, 26:314-26.

Bhutta ZA et al. Evidence-based interventions for improvement of maternal and child nutrition: what can be done and at what cost? Lancet. 2013, S0140-6736(13)60996-4.

Imdad A, Yakoob MY, Bhutta ZA. Effect of breastfeeding promotion interventions on breastfeeding rates, with special focus on developing countries. BMC Public Health. 2011, 11 Suppl 3:S24.

Davies-Adetugbo AA, et al. Breast-feeding promotion in a diarrhoea programme in rural communities. Journal of Diarrhoeal Disease Research. 1997,15:161-6.

Morrow AL, et al. Efficacy of home-based peer counselling to promote exclusive breastfeeding: a randomised controlled trial. Lancet. 1999, 353:1226-31.

Haider R, et al. Effect of community-based peer counsellors on exclusive breastfeeding practices in Dhaka, Bangladesh: a randomised controlled trial. Lancet. 2000,356:1643-7.

Bhandari N, et al. Effect of community-based promotion of exclusive breastfeeding on diarrhoeal illness and growth: a cluster randomised controlled trial. Lancet. 2003,361:1418-23.

Aidam BA, Pérez-Escamilla R, Lartey A. Lactation counseling increases exclusive breast-feeding rates in Ghana. Journal of Nutrition. 2005,135:1691-5.

Tylleskär T, et al. Exclusive breastfeeding promotion by peer counsellors in sub-Saharan Africa (PROMISE-EBF): a cluster-randomised trial. Lancet. 2011,378:420-7.

# REFERENCES

Quinn VJ, et al. Improving breastfeeding practices on a broad scale at the community level: success stories from Africa and Latin America. Journal of Human Lactation. 2005,21:345-54.

Baker EJ, Sanei LC, Franklin N. Early initiation of and exclusive breastfeeding in large-scale community-based programmes in Bolivia and Madagascar. Journal of Health and Population Nutrition. 2006, 24:530-9.

Guyon AB, et al. Implementing an integrated nutrition package at large scale in Madagascar: the Essential Nutrition Actions framework. Food and Nutrition Bulletin. 2009,30:233-44.

Fadnes LT, et al. Need to optimise infant feeding counselling: a cross-sectional survey among HIV-positive mothers in Eastern Uganda. BMC Pediatrics. 2009,9:2.

Doherty T, et al. Early cessation of breastfeeding amongst women in South Africa: an area needing urgent attention to improve child health. BMC Pediatrics. 2012,12:105.

Doherty T, Sanders D, Goga A, Jackson D. Implications of the new WHO guidelines on HIV and infant feeding for child survival in South Africa. Bulletin of the World Health Organization. 2011,89:62-7.

Renfrew M, et al. Addressing a learning deficit in breastfeeding: strategies for change. Maternal and Child Nutrition. 2006,2:239-44.

Disclaimer:
The named authors alone are responsible for the views expressed in this document.

Declarations of interests:
Conflict of interest statements were collected from all named authors and no conflicts were identified.

# About the Author

Charlee King's success as a serial entrepreneur, health professional, author, national public speaker, and advocate has earned her features and recognition with major media platforms and organizations.

Having carved out an impressive niche in the confection world on a national level as owner of the booming baking business Mommy's Sweet Treats, she has been deemed the "Cookie Queen." The concept of this cookie enterprise was birthed through her own personal challenges with milk production after the birth of her daughter and the difficulty in receiving the proper support and knowledge. Her purpose as a respected health professional combined with this entrepreneur endeavor raises awareness in areas where this vital health information for mothers and families is not readily available.

With her mission being moms, she is the author of Thanks for Telling Me, a compassionate but comical guide for mothers, mothers to be, and women considering motherhood addressing the unforeseen changes their little bundle of joy can bring to their body and emotions through intimate accounts and education. With wittiness and wisdom, King is that much needed "Mommy Mentor," preparing women for the process of pregnancy and post labor. Her knowledge affords her opportunities to speak and instruct on breastfeeding and similar topics relevant to mothers on platforms nationwide. Though she appreciates her accolades and attainments, she boasts that her greatest accomplishment is being a mother.

www.ingramcontent.com/pod-product-compliance
Lightning Source LLC
Chambersburg PA
CBHW070335230426
43663CB00011B/2328